This awesome activity book is bursting
with activities to choose from.
From coloring and doodling
to dot to dots, sudoku, and
brain-teaser puzzles, it's time to pick
an activity and have some fun!
You can check all your answers to the
puzzles at the back of the book.

What are you waiting for?

Silver Dolphin

Silver Dolphin Books
An imprint of Printers Row Publishing Group
A division of Readerlink Distribution Services, LLC
10350 Barnes Canyon Road, Suite 100, San Diego, CA 92121
www.silverdolphinbooks.com

Compilation copyright © 2016, 2014 Buster Books
Illustrations and layouts © 2014, 2013, 2012, 2011, 2009, 2008, 2006, 2005 Buster Books

Printers Row Publishing Group is a division of Readerlink Distribution Services, LLC.
Silver Dolphin Books is a registered trademark of Readerlink Distribution Services, LLC.

Designed by Jack Clucas
Edited by Hannah Cohen
Illustrations by Hannah Davies, Andrew Pinder, and Emily Golden Twomey
Word search and crossword puzzles and solutions by Dr Gareth Moore
Puzzles designed and typeset by Gareth Moore www.drgarethmoore.com
Sudoku puzzles and solutions by Alastair Chisholm

Wordsearch and crossword puzzles and solutions © 2011 Gareth Moore
Sudoku puzzles and solutions copyright © 2005 Alastair Chisholm

This book contains material previously published in
The Kids' Book of Crosswords, The Kids' Book of Wordsearches, Dot To Dot,
Buster's Brilliant Dot To Dot, Colour By Numbers, Buster's Brilliant Colour By Numbers,
The Kids' Book of Sudoku Book 1, The Girls' Fabulous Colouring Book,
The Girls' Glorious Colouring Book, The Boys' Doodle Book 2, and *The Girls' Doodle Book 2*
With additional material adapted from www.shutterstock.com

All notations of errors or omissions should be addressed to Silver Dolphin Books,
Editorial Department, at the above address. All other correspondence (author inquiries,
permissions) concerning the content of this book should be addressed to:
Buster Books, an imprint of Michael O'Mara Books Ltd,
9 Lion Yard, Tremadoc Road, London SW4 7NQ.
www.busterbooks.co.uk

ISBN: 978-1-62686-733-8

Manufactured, printed, and assembled in Dongguan, China.
Seventh printing, June 2020. RRD/06/20
24 23 22 21 20 7 8 9 10 11

1 = purple   2 = red   3 = blue   4 = yellow   5 = green   6 = pink   7 = orange
8 = brown   9 = white

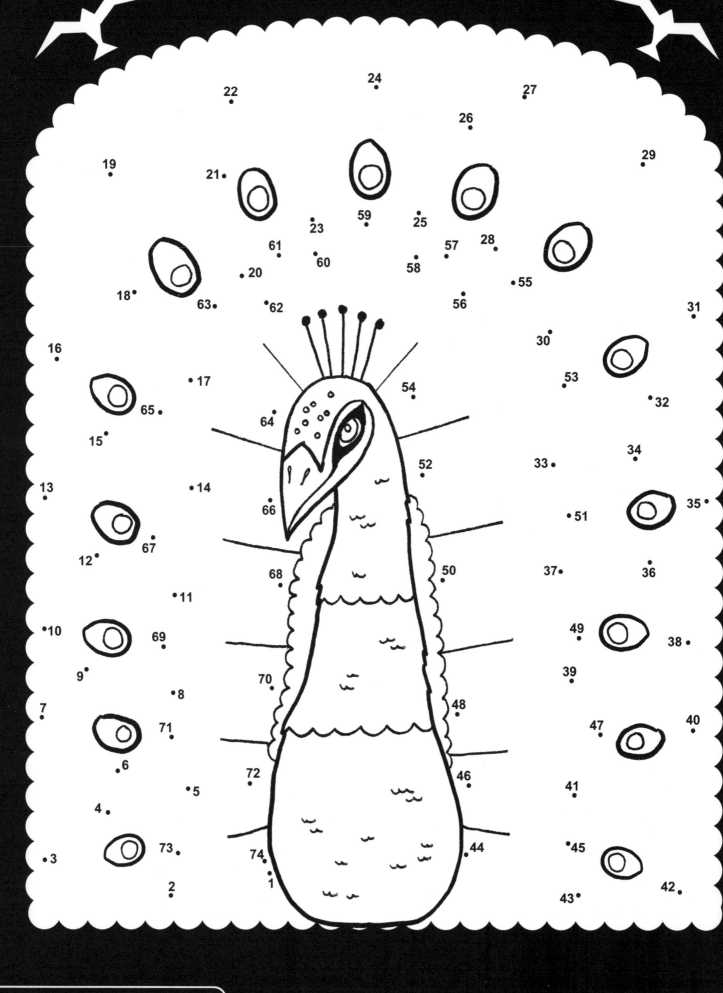

What an enormous whale!

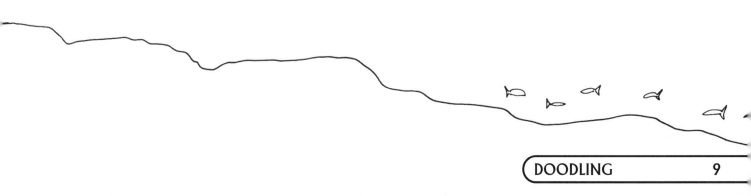

COLORING

CROSSWORDS

The crosswords in this section will test your word power. The rules are very simple: just find the solution word described by each numbered across or down clue and then write it into the corresponding squares in the grid. Sometimes, you will be able to think of more than one solution to a clue. When this happens, wait until you solve some of the words that cross over that one in the grid, then use these to help you choose the correct solution.

Each clue has a number in brackets at the end, like this: (4). This shows you how many letters are in the word you are trying to guess and matches the number of empty squares in the grid. Occasionally you might see two numbers, like this: (3, 3). This means there are two words to place, each of the given length, such as "The End." Don't leave a space between the words in the grid, though–write one letter in each square. If you see a ";" in a clue, it means the clue is made up of different parts which will help you guess the solution. For example, the clue: "Opposite of front; rear of your body (4)" provides two clues for "back."

If you get completely stuck, don't worry–all of the answers are in the back of the book.

Puzzle: 1

Across
1 Large, edible fish with pink flesh (6)
4 Useful (7)
6 Leafy, green vegetable that Popeye eats (7)
8 Hang or swing loosely (6)

Down
1 Clean the floor with a broom (5)
2 Part of the body; one circuit of a track (3)
3 A score of nothing in a football match (3)
5 Parent's brother (5)
6 Not happy (3)
7 Pester or repeatedly complain to someone (3)

Puzzle: 2

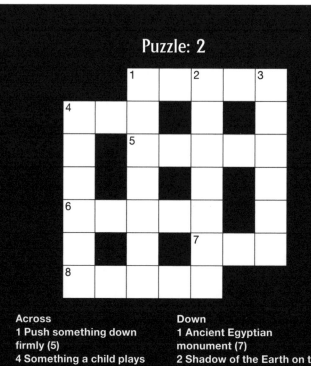

Across
1 Push something down firmly (5)
4 Something a child plays with (3)
5 Turns over and over (5)
6 Add some numbers (3,2)
7 A knight's title, ___ Galahad, for example (3)
8 Deep spoon with long handle, often used to serve soup (5)

Down
1 Ancient Egyptian monument (7)
2 Shadow of the Earth on the moon (7)
3 Female sibling (6)
4 Glittery material used to decorate Christmas trees (6)

Puzzle: 3

Across
2 Plan or diagram; a pie _____ (5)
4 Diary to write thoughts in (7)
5 Tap on a door (5)

Down
1 Another word for a soldier or fighter (7)
2 Something that tells the time (5)
3 Something trains run on (5)

Puzzle: 4

Across
1 Get pleasure from (5)
3 The cover over a building (4)
5 Hover in the air (5)
8 Someone who travels in a spaceship (9)
9 Sharp point growing on a rose stem (5)
11 Noise made by a clock (4)
12 Opposite of loud (5)

Down
1 Small mischievous fairy (3)
2 Whirlwind (7)
4 Something that is true (4)
6 Large bird that can run fast but can't fly (7)
7 Edible freshwater fish (5)
8 Parent's sister (4)
10 Something used to catch fish with (3)

Puzzle: 5

Across
2 Superhero's cloak (4)
4 Person who does something brave (4)
5 An army officer of high rank (5)
6 For example: kitchen, lounge or hall (4)
7 Lazy (4)

Down
1 Mythical creature with a woman's body and a fish's tail (7)
2 Perform a magic trick (7)
3 Ancient Egyptian king (7)

Puzzle: 6

Across
1 Small, dark red fruit on a stalk with a stone in the center (6)
4 Long, stringy food served with many Asian meals (7)
6 Take your clothes off (7)
8 The white surface of teeth (6)

Down
1 Might go on a Queen's head (5)
2 The point where something stops (3)
3 Word for agreeing (3)
5 Stand used by artist to hold a canvas while painting (5)
6 Utilize something (3)
7 Male sheep (3)

Puzzle: 7

Across
1 Fading light in the early evening (4)
3 What you might call a male teacher (3)
5 Spoon used for serving soft food, such as ice cream (5)
6 Sharp cutting tool (5)
7 Utter a word or sentence (3)
8 Not pleasant to look at (4)

Down
1 A heavy disk thrown during athletic events (6)
2 Ghostly; creepy (6)
3 Coiled spiral of metal wire, often found in a mattress (6)
4 Cure for an illness (6)

Puzzle: 8

Across
1 Noise made by a duck (5)
5 Person being treated by a doctor (7)
6 Toy with two wheels that you ride (7)
7 Small garden ornament with beard and pointed hat (5)

Down
2 Standard outfit everyone at the same place wears (7)
3 Decide not to do something; an on-screen button to say "no" to an option (6)
4 Small type of hawk (6)

Puzzle: 9

Across
3 Used for taking photographs (6)
4 In support of (3)
5 Untidy; dirty (5)
7 Male pig (3)
8 Voucher (6)

Down
1 Female horse (4)
2 Wax coloring item (6)
3 Ordinary; usual (6)
6 Outer covering for your foot (4)

Puzzle: 10

Across
2 Food selected to help someone become healthier (4)
4 String used to tie up a shoe (4)
5 Fourth month (5)
6 Loose earth (4)
7 Grated peel of a lemon or orange (4)

Down
1 Singing along and following words on a screen (7)
2 Unfreeze (7)
3 To shout or speak suddenly (7)

Puzzle: 11

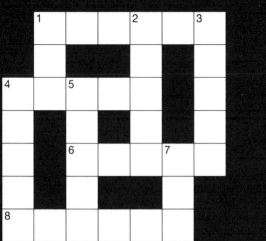

Across
1 Prehistoric animal remains found in rock (6)
4 Precious stone (5)
6 Newly made (5)
8 Sadness (6)

Down
1 Payment; charge (3)
2 Work out a solution (5)
3 Meal at midday (5)
4 Pants made of denim (5)
5 Thin biscuit (5)
7 Noticed something, as in "I ___ it happen" (3)

Puzzle: 12

Across
1 Instrument often pictured being played by angels (4)
4 Tear something, such as a piece of paper (3)
6 Male who delivers letters (7)
7 Container for storing trash (3)
8 Be brave enough to do something (4)

Down
2 Soak up some liquid (6)
3 Imagine something is real (7)
5 Words you address to God (6)

Puzzle: 13

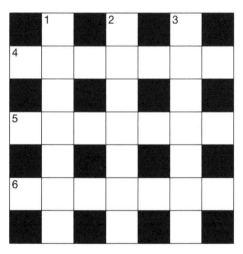

Across
4 Machine for carrying people or goods (7)
5 Warm up your muscles before exercise (7)
6 Thin, crispy biscuit (7)

Down
1 The characters that make up the alphabet (7)
2 Absolute quiet (7)
3 Slow-moving mass of ice found on land (7)

Puzzle: 14

Across
3 People who catch criminals (6)
4 Female parent (3)
5 A time without war (5)
7 Not strict (3)
8 A light gas used to fill floating balloons (6)

Down
1 Tall, rounded roof (4)
2 Loud, shrill cry (6)
3 Doll controlled by hand, sometimes with strings (6)
6 A group where people enjoy the same hobby; black playing card (4)

Puzzle: 15

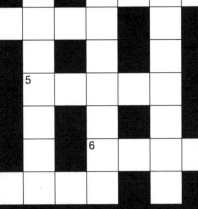

Across
2 Notice board; in astrology, which star ____ are you? (4)
4 A walking track (4)
5 The overall amount (5)
6 Organ used for breathing (4)
7 Very tall plant with branches and leaves (4)

Down
1 Big black leopard (7)
2 Vehicle traveling back and forth (7)
3 A wreath of flowers worn around the neck or hung up (7)

Puzzle: 16

Across
1 On time; without delay (6)
4 Opposite of light (5)
6 Before all the others (5)
8 Primary painting color (6)

Down
1 Dessert usually filled with fruit (3)
2 Person in charge of a town (5)
3 Grilled bread (5)
4 Cheery; contented (5)
5 Very bad (5)
7 Female pig (3)

Puzzle: 17

Across
3 Soft floor covering (6)
4 Reddish, dog-like animal (3)
5 Small fairy (5)
7 Opposite of wet (3)
8 Something you must keep to yourself (6)

Down
1 A cab (4)
2 Large area of dry land, often covered in sand (6)
3 Red-brown metal used in wires (6)
6 Thought (4)

Puzzle: 18

Across
1 Instructions for cooking food (6)
4 Greet on arrival (7)
5 Unusual; different (7)
7 Long-stemmed, crunchy green vegetable, often eaten raw (6)

Down
1 Not cooked (3)
2 School for continuing education (7)
3 Say that you will definitely do something (7)
6 Produce an egg, if you're a hen (3)

Puzzle: 19

Across
1 To handle a situation (4)
3 Said to someone when you leave them (3)
5 Woolly animal, like a smaller camel without a hump (5)
6 Joint of your arm (5)
7 For example: brazil, hazel, almond (3)
8 Pull something heavy (4)

Down
1 Pillar, often found in Greek and Roman ruins (6)
2 For example: Earth, Jupiter or Mars (6)
3 Hairdresser for men (6)
4 Small crawling insect with pincers (6)

Puzzle: 20

Across
1 Not very happy (5)
5 Someone who visits places abroad (7)
6 Spectacles (7)
7 The measurement between two lines that meet at a point (5)

Down
2 Light umbrella used in the sunshine (7)
3 Christian festival during spring (6)
4 Powder inside a flower (6)

Puzzle: 21

Across
3 About the sea; name for a soldier serving on board a ship (6)
4 Object used to cool yourself (3)
5 Raised platform for theater shows (5)
7 Covered in ice (3)
8 The opposite of arrive (6)

Down
1 Feel you would like something, as in "I _ _ _ _ this" (4)
2 Small creature with six legs (6)
3 Man in charge (6)
6 Female child (4)

Puzzle: 22

Across
2 Circular device found on cars (5)
4 Something old and valuable (7)
5 Time when you are young; type of club for young people (5)

Down
1 Not funny (7)
2 Blustery, as in "this is _ _ _ _ _ weather" (5)
3 Giggle (5)

WORD SEARCHES

This section is full of word searches. Beneath each puzzle is a list of words that are hidden in the grid above it. You'll find the words running in a straight line in any direction, including diagonally, and either forwards or backwards.

Occasionally, some of the puzzles contain a phrase or word written beneath the grid that includes punctuation–in these cases just ignore the spaces or punctuation marks when looking in the grid. When you find a word, mark it in the grid and cross it off the list below. Some of the puzzles have interesting shapes with lines drawn between the letters in the grid–ignore these when solving the puzzles, since the words can still run across these lines.

You should also remember that some of the words in each puzzle will overlap one another–using the same letters in the grid.

If you get completely stuck and can't find a word, don't worry–all of the answers are in the back of the book.

Puzzle 1: Let's Face It

```
I  H  D  C  E  I  T  E  Y  E
R  S  A  S  G  S  C  H  H  H
E  S  E  C  N  E  T  M  N  H
O  Y  H  H  O  K  O  T  S  N
E  I  E  C  S  U  E  C  K  T
N  E  R  B  T  A  Y  H  E  O
N  T  O  H  R  S  L  E  I  N
O  R  F  S  I  O  T  E  W  G
M  D  H  E  L  H  W  K  Y  U
E  E  N  O  S  E  S  S  K  E
```

CHEEKS	FOREHEAD
CHIN	MOUTH
EARS	NOSE
EYEBROWS	NOSTRILS
EYELASHES	TEETH
EYES	TONGUE

Puzzle 2: Animal Safari

```
            A  H  G  N  U  S
         W  I  I  C  I  K  U  E
         L  A  P  P  I  R  M  N
         E  A  N  I  A  R  A  E
         W  T  K  T  E  K  T  F
R  H  I  N  O  C  E  R  O  S  F  O
H  Y  L  A  E  K  A  L  P  R  O  E
O  E  D  H  T  O  E  J  O  A  Y  H
F  N  D  P  A  A  T  R  P  P  N  X
F  A  O  E  Y  D  R  A  P  O  E  L
         G  L         R  I
         C  E         L  H
```

ANTELOPE	LEOPARD
ELEPHANT	LION
HIPPOPOTAMUS	OKAPI
HYENA	ORYX
GIRAFFE	OSTRICH
GNU	RHINOCEROS
JACKAL	WILD DOG

Puzzle 3: Playing Chess

```
D A E P N R
R B T W I N
A E A G C E
O P M C A A
B O K I A M S B P G
S H C A T P B T N S
S S E H C Z T I L B
E I H R O O K U T E
H B C R E T I B R A
C T N A S S A P N E
```

BISHOP   GAMBIT
BLITZ CHESS   KING
CAPTURE   PAWN
CASTLE   ROOK
CHECKMATE   TIMER
CHESSBOARD   WIN

Puzzle 4: Medical Attention

```
        G T M R
        P A R E
        U B C T
        R L I S
Y E M G Y E T A L R B S
A D U O S T O L N U N T
P R E S C R I P T I O N
D E E M S P B P M O E E
        E I I A
        E R T C
        Y I N Y
        V R A I
```

ANTIBIOTIC   REMEDY
DRUG   SYRUP
PILL   TABLET
PLASTER   TISSUE
PRESCRIPTION VITAMINS

Puzzle 5: Time for Fun

```
G L L A B T O O F V
M R E A D I N G T C
S W R I T I N G O G
E I N D L I N M N E
L A S A T I P I A I
Z I Z N H U M L O L
Z E I C T M
U A T E I R
P A R W I L
W S S T C D
```

ART   PAINTING   WATCHING TV
COMPUTERS PUZZLES   WRITING
DANCE   READING
FOOTBALL   SWIMMING

Puzzle 6: Numbers, Big and Small

```
N N E S E V L E W T
I E I N I O H L T H
T N Y N W X E E X O
W L E T E E T V N U
S E V E N T E E N S
T H I R T E E N E A
        U H W E T N
        T O G T N D
        Y T F I F N
        T F I V E W
```

EIGHTEEN   NINETEEN   THOUSAND
ELEVEN   ONE   TWELVE
FIFTY   SEVENTEEN   TWENTY
FIVE   SIXTEEN   TWO
FOUR   THIRTEEN

Puzzle 7: Things You Put On the Wall

```
N P G P R E T S O P
W G N L H D E Y H W
I N I A L R R O A K
N I V S U T T L K O
D T O T S O L R W O
O N C E G P O N N H
W I P R A W
P A A P T I
T P E R P P
H R A E S T
```

ARTWORK
HOOK
PAINTING
PHOTOGRAPH
PICTURE
PLASTER

POSTER
SIGN
TAPESTRY
WALLPAPER
WINDOW

Puzzle 8: Fluffy Animals

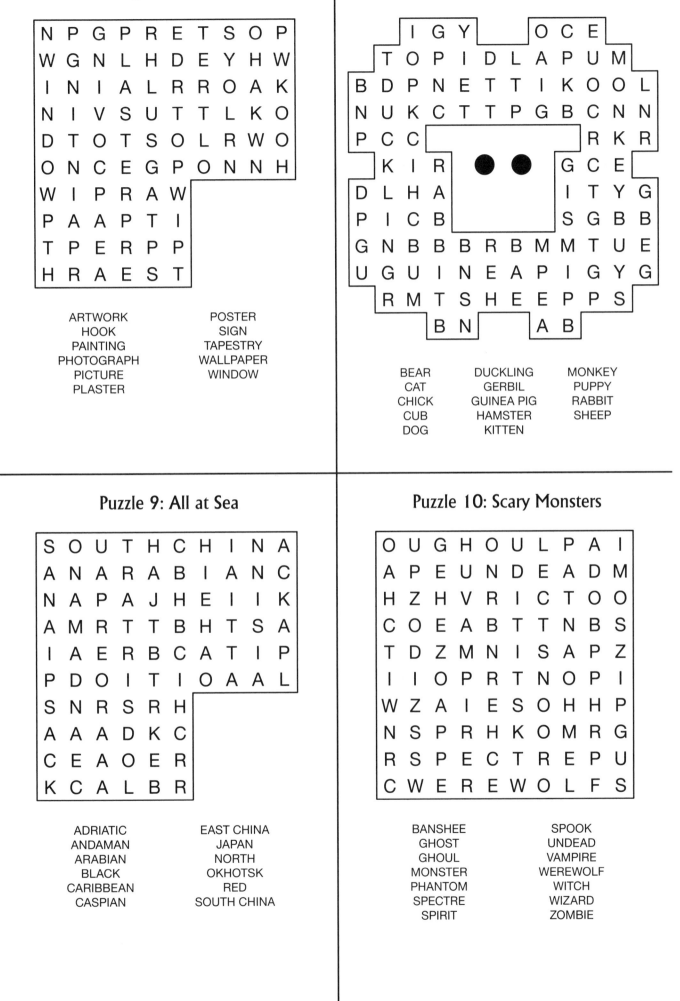

```
        I G Y       O C E
    T O P I D L A P U M
  B D P N E T T I K O O L
  N U K C T T P G B C N N
  P C C                 R K R
  K I R    ●   ●    G C E
  D L H A           I T Y G
  P I C B           S G B B
  G N B B B R B M M T U E
  U G U I N E A P I G Y G
    R M T S H E E P P S
      B N       A B
```

BEAR
CAT
CHICK
CUB
DOG

DUCKLING
GERBIL
GUINEA PIG
HAMSTER
KITTEN

MONKEY
PUPPY
RABBIT
SHEEP

Puzzle 9: All at Sea

```
S O U T H C H I N A
A N A R A B I A N C
N A P A J H E I I K
A M R T T B H T S A
I A E R B C A T I P
P D O I T I O A A L
S N R S R H
A A A D K C
C E A O E R
K C A L B R
```

ADRIATIC
ANDAMAN
ARABIAN
BLACK
CARIBBEAN
CASPIAN

EAST CHINA
JAPAN
NORTH
OKHOTSK
RED
SOUTH CHINA

Puzzle 10: Scary Monsters

```
O U G H O U L P A I
A P E U N D E A D M
H Z H V R I C T O O
C O E A B T T N B S
T D Z M N I S A P Z
I I O P R T N O P I
W Z A I E S O H H P
N S P R H K O M R G
R S P E C T R E P U
C W E R E W O L F S
```

BANSHEE
GHOST
GHOUL
MONSTER
PHANTOM
SPECTRE
SPIRIT

SPOOK
UNDEAD
VAMPIRE
WEREWOLF
WITCH
WIZARD
ZOMBIE

Puzzle 11: Dinner Time

```
        A S R U P O U F
        S N U S Z H U I
        P Y R F R I T S
        R A U D S T A H
A A T R U A U S E N M A
Y Z U A Y N Y H T O N N
E C Z S P G G P U O S D
S H A I U A S S S D U C
N E N T P S S K A L R H
P E S S R A H T L E N I
P E H U K L U I A S G P
O T S A O R Y A D N U S
```

CURRY	PASTA	SUNDAY
FISH AND	PIZZA	ROAST
CHIPS	SALAD	SUSHI
LASAGNA	SOUP	TAPAS
MOUSSAKA	SPAGHETTI	
NOODLES	STIR FRY	

Puzzle 12: They're All Teachers!

```
C S R E T S A M D A E H
R L E C T U R E R R R E
O A         T N R R E A
R P         N O O P C D
E I         R L R D O M
N C         L O E C A I
I N R L I E F A T E C S
A I T S S E N O C A H T
R R I N S T R U C T O R
T P U S T E A C H E R E
I O O R W O L L E F D S
C R R G O V E R N E S S
```

COACH	HEADMASTER	PROFESSOR
DEAN	HEADMISTRESS	TEACHER
DOCTOR	INSTRUCTOR	TRAINER
FELLOW	LECTURER	TUTOR
GOVERNESS	PRINCIPAL	

Puzzle 13: Fish for Dinner

```
A P M I R            T
E L A G          U M
R M A N        O A I
C O D I G C R C P M
H N ● T C L T K J O E
N A A I E E E E L N L
J O H N D O R Y K O L U
W M L U E F F S S A B
A L L T I        D C F
C A S S          K G
H S H S          T
O L A I W
```

ANGLER FISH	MONKFISH	SOLE
BASS	PERCH	TROUT
COD	PLAICE	TUNA
JOHN DORY	POLLACK	WHITING
MACKEREL	SALMON	

Puzzle 14: Juicy Jumble

```
E E P A L M T R O E
Y G I O O A I O O P
A R N O N N U N G F
W H E A T G R A S S
    L A L R O F B S
    I P A E O N E G
    M P G O C O E I
    E L U S A I T N
      E A R R S R
      M V S R S O
      O A E O A O
      N V A T P T
```

BEETROOT	LIME
CARROT	MANGO
CELERY	ORANGE
GRAPE	PASSION FRUIT
GUAVA	PINEAPPLE
LEMON	WHEATGRASS

Puzzle 15: Gamers' Corner

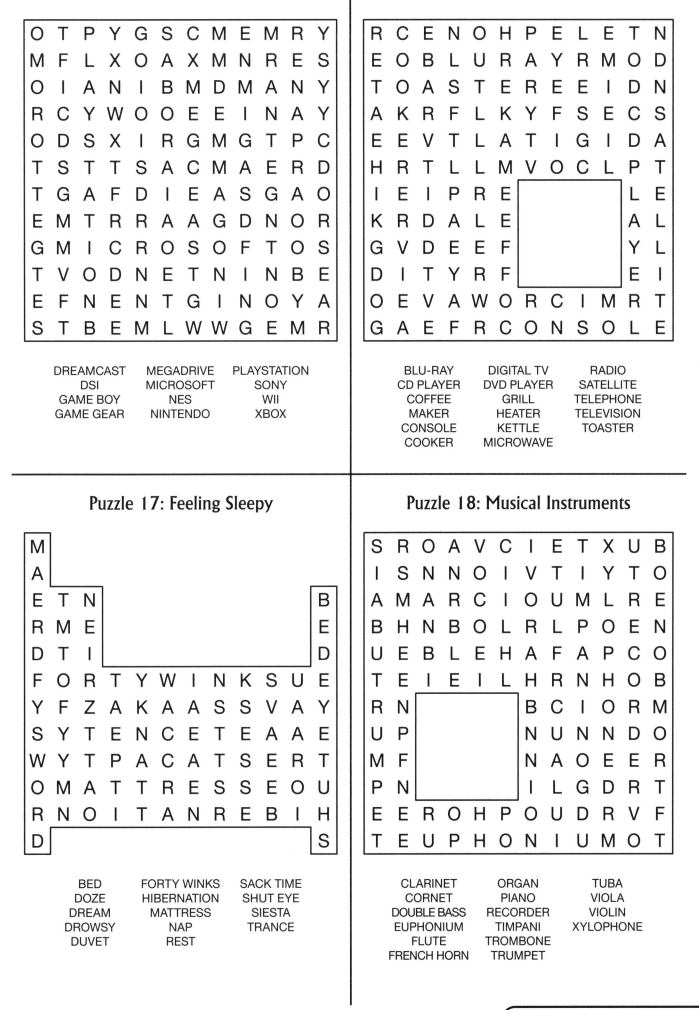

```
O T P Y G S C M E M R Y
M F L X O A X M N R E S
O I A N I B M D M A N Y
R C Y W O O E E I N A Y
O D S X I R G M G T P C
T S T T S A C M A E R D
T G A F D I E A S G A O
E M T R R A A G D N O R
G M I C R O S O F T O S
T V O D N E T N I N B E
E F N E N T G I N O Y A
S T B E M L W W G E M R
```

DREAMCAST	MEGADRIVE	PLAYSTATION
DSI	MICROSOFT	SONY
GAME BOY	NES	WII
GAME GEAR	NINTENDO	XBOX

Puzzle 16: Plug-In Equipment

```
R C E N O H P E L E T N
E O B L U R A Y R M O D
T O A S T E R E E I D N
A K R F L K Y F S E C S
E E V T L A T I G I D A
H R T L L M V O C L P T
I E I P R E        L E
K R D A L E        A L
G V D E E F        Y L
D I T Y R F        E I
O E V A W O R C I M R T
G A E F R C O N S O L E
```

BLU-RAY	DIGITAL TV	RADIO
CD PLAYER	DVD PLAYER	SATELLITE
COFFEE	GRILL	TELEPHONE
MAKER	HEATER	TELEVISION
CONSOLE	KETTLE	TOASTER
COOKER	MICROWAVE	

Puzzle 17: Feeling Sleepy

```
M
A
E T N             B
R M E             E
D T I             D
F O R T Y W I N K S U E
Y F Z A K A A S S V A Y
S Y T E N C E T E A A E
W Y T P A C A T S E R T
O M A T T R E S S E O U
R N O I T A N R E B I H
D                   S
```

BED	FORTY WINKS	SACK TIME
DOZE	HIBERNATION	SHUT EYE
DREAM	MATTRESS	SIESTA
DROWSY	NAP	TRANCE
DUVET	REST	

Puzzle 18: Musical Instruments

```
S R O A V C I E T X U B
I S N N O I V T I Y T O
A M A R C I O U M L R E
B H N B O L R L P O E N
U E B L E H A F A P C O
T E I E I L H R N H O B
R N       B C I O R M
U P       N U N N D O
M F       N A O E E R
P N       I L G D R T
E E R O H P O U D R V F
T E U P H O N I U M O T
```

CLARINET	ORGAN	TUBA
CORNET	PIANO	VIOLA
DOUBLE BASS	RECORDER	VIOLIN
EUPHONIUM	TIMPANI	XYLOPHONE
FLUTE	TROMBONE	
FRENCH HORN	TRUMPET	

Puzzle 19: Brass Instruments

```
N U U M G U N R U R G N
R R T R U M P E T R T R
H B O E E I T E R T O H
N R O H H C N E R F U T
O R R G L O L O N M G E
O G P F R E M O H R R E
T E T H O B G P E P O U
T E O T O P U U O N U C
T R R N N E H G L R P E
N U E H R N R O L F L M
N I M O U P E H M E G M
T R L O L H R G T R U H
```

BUGLE
CORNET
EUPHONIUM
FLUGELHORN
FRENCH HORN
TENOR HORN
TROMBONE
TRUMPET

Puzzle 20: Magic Tricks

```
I D O D          C D I D
      C           H
      A O P T
      A P A I D L
      S E O R N R
F L A H N I W A S D H I
      N H D B W E
      S S B E C V
      C I D I I O
      T N D R G L
      R A B O A G
      S V H L M C
```

CAPE
CARDS
COINS
DICE
GLOVES
HAT
MAGIC WAND
RABBIT
SAW IN HALF
VANISH

Puzzle 21: In the Kitchen

```
P K N I F E R G E S N E
P U G I G J U U R S S P
R A C R P S A J E E E S
E E L G A G N G V R L T
X N N U N T N N A P A R
I N O E T I E I E C C A
M A L O P A R R L I S I
R R C A P O P U C L O N
      D S N S S R O E
      I L A A I A N R
      N P E E C G E T
      I I E M T P R M
```

CAN OPENER
CLEAVER
GARLIC PRESS
GRATER
KNIFE
LADLE
MEASURING CUP
MEASURING JUG
MIXER
ROLLING PIN
SCALES
SPATULA
STRAINER
TEASPOON

Puzzle 22: Month Mix-Up

```
T R J A N U A R Y A
S E P T E M B E R P
M B Y R A U R B E F
P O F         M B L
H T A         E M A
A C P         C E U
J O R         E V G
R U I A A R N D O U
U M L E M U G U N S
A M A Y J E U T S T
```

APRIL
AUGUST
DECEMBER
FEBRUARY
JANUARY
JULY
JUNE
MARCH
MAY
NOVEMBER
OCTOBER
SEPTEMBER

Puzzle 23: In the Bathroom

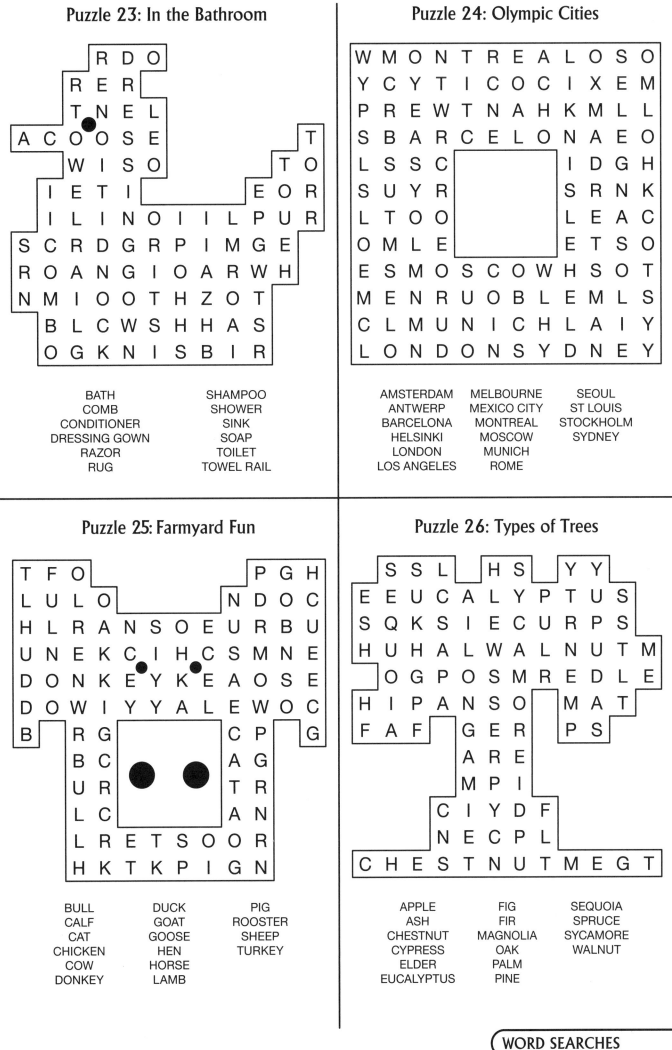

```
      R D O
    R E R     L
    T N E     L
A C O O S E
    W I S O         T
    I E T I       T O
    I L I N O I I L P U R
  S C R D G R P I M G E
  R O A N G I O A R W H
  N M I O O T H Z O T
    B L C W S H H A S
    O G K N I S B I R
```

BATH · COMB · CONDITIONER · DRESSING GOWN · RAZOR · RUG · SHAMPOO · SHOWER · SINK · SOAP · TOILET · TOWEL RAIL

Puzzle 24: Olympic Cities

```
W M O N T R E A L O S O
Y C Y T I C O C I X E M
P R E W T N A H K M L L
S B A R C E L O N A E O
L S S C         I D G H
S U Y R         S R N K
L T O O         L E A C
O M L E         E T S O
E S M O S C O W H S O T
M E N R U O B L E M L S
C L M U N I C H L A I Y
L O N D O N S Y D N E Y
```

AMSTERDAM · ANTWERP · BARCELONA · HELSINKI · LONDON · LOS ANGELES · MELBOURNE · MEXICO CITY · MONTREAL · MOSCOW · MUNICH · ROME · SEOUL · ST LOUIS · STOCKHOLM · SYDNEY

Puzzle 25: Farmyard Fun

```
T F O           P G H
L U L O       N D O C
H L R A N S O E U R B U
U N E K C I H C S M N E
D O N K E Y K E A O S E
D O W I Y Y A L E W O C
B   R G       C P   G
    B C       A G
    U R       T R
    L C       A N
    L R E T S O O R
    H K T K P I G N
```

BULL · CALF · CAT · CHICKEN · COW · DONKEY · DUCK · GOAT · GOOSE · HEN · HORSE · LAMB · PIG · ROOSTER · SHEEP · TURKEY

Puzzle 26: Types of Trees

```
  S S L   H S   Y Y
E E U C A L Y P T U S
S Q K S I E C U R P S
H U H A L W A L N U T M
  O G P O S M R E D L E
  H I P A N S O   M A T
  F A F   G E R   P S
        A R E
        M P I
      C I Y D F
      N E C P L
C H E S T N U T M E G T
```

APPLE · ASH · CHESTNUT · CYPRESS · ELDER · EUCALYPTUS · FIG · FIR · MAGNOLIA · OAK · PALM · PINE · SEQUOIA · SPRUCE · SYCAMORE · WALNUT

Puzzle 27: Orchestral Instruments

```
E N I I S P A N P E T I
A T N A O C R V R L O L
I N U N E T I D A L I L
V I O L I N R O H A O T
P T L O F O O U S O O A
S O F T S P T B M L T V
P L T F I S O L M P I A
P R O O I M A E E O E V
O E L S E E P B L C R T
M B T E N I R A L C T T
M S O C E N O S N N C R
N S P E R C U S S I O N
```

BASSOON   HARP   TROMBONE
CELLO   HORN   TRUMPET
CLARINET   OBOE   VIOLA
DOUBLE BASS   PERCUSSION   VIOLIN
FLUTE   TIMPANI

Puzzle 28: Toy Box

```
          E
        T Z L
      L R I S Z
    N A A L K J Z
  N Y N I L U I A U
S P I N N I N G T O P
  R K L S L S S L E
  Y A A E Z L A O C
    T C T D L W A
      O Y Z O R
        L O O D M
          N S T
```

CARDS   PUZZLE
DOLLS   SLINKY
JIGSAW   SPINNING TOP
KITE   TOY CARS
MODEL   TRAIN SET

Puzzle 29: Board Games

```
I B S N B R M O U T O M C A
A T O U T A E L E T S J O L
E R A F H E C V U A O C N S
B P G J I E N K E D M O N S
Y C O D A E M C G R O D E M
B N T N B       A S N C T
G H M C M       U M I T S
C S I O P       G G M F B
R K V N N       H O R O O
C E O C H O S E B T H E U N
C T C M H A P S M S A T R M
O G S E U E E O D L E S C D
O N H P I H S E L T T A B G
E A V R R C M S T Y M M N G
```

BACKGAMMON   FOUR   MASTERMIND
BATTLESHIP   DRAUGHTS   MONOPOLY
CHESS   LUDO   REVERSI
CONNECT FOUR   MAH-JONG

Puzzle 30: Capital Cities

```
S S B T C          N B M W C
I T E S E          A L A C A
R O L E M          I S D O I
A C G P K          R N R P R
P K R A G O B S A O E E E O
H H A D I R K W T B H T N A
E O D U O T U G P I T S H R
L L E B P L N O N A A M A R
S M A D D I S A B A B A G E
I C I M H H S O S M B E E B
N H U S I H L E D W E N N N
K U A L A L U M P U R X A A
I W E L L I N G T O N A U C
S L E S S U R B T K E L O L
```

ADDIS ABABA   CANBERRA   PARIS
AMSTERDAM   COPENHAGEN   SANTIAGO
ATHENS   HELSINKI   STOCKHOLM
BANGKOK   KUALA LUMPUR   WARSAW
BELGRADE   LIMA   WASHINGTON
BERNE   LUXEMBOURG   DC
BRUSSELS   NAIROBI   WELLINGTON
BUDAPEST   NEW DELHI
CAIRO   OSLO

Puzzle 31: Didn't Do My Homework

```
S N I A R T N O T F E L K T
W R E D O G A T E I T N W I
E E I M D O A A N I I I O K
R P Y O O N T N O S K O D O
I A H T D H E D N O O L N O
F P S P I L T I N K O N I T
T F R W O N D A D S T T W D
H O B T D E D S T T R E T N
G T S L P A O M O I E E U E
U U P E D Y O L K T S O I
A O O N N B B I R B S F W R
C R A N O U T O F T I M E F
D I O O S F P T T F S W L L
B I K Y T Y A W A W E L B D
```

BLEW AWAY
BLEW OUT WINDOW
CAUGHT FIRE
COULDN'T DO IT
DOG ATE IT
DROPPED IN SINK
FRIEND TOOK IT
LEFT IT AT HOME

LEFT ON TRAIN
LOST MY BOOK
OUT OF PAPER
RAN OUT OF TIME
SISTER TOOK IT
SPILT INK ON IT
STOLEN
TOO BUSY

Puzzle 32: Cat Breeds

```
Y E S N L E T S Y E S C A B
B Y B Y A T S E M M I R Y B
T O R T O I S E S H E L L K
B N R M I T N I M B I A B M
E E T A N N A I S R E P N G
E S O I S M I B S T U X N B
Y P Y A E L R A B S N B P S
N Y G S S N E S I Y Y B N H
Y E E T T E B T H L E B C R
B X R M E O I P E E L B A I
S O T A M O S E B A H G Y E
E B S B A O A O C E B A I C
X N A M I O N K N A M A O A
K Y B I N U C M M O I R L T
```

ABYSSINIAN
BLACK
BOMBAY
BURMESE
MANX
PERSIAN

SIAMESE
SIBERIAN
SPHYNX
TABBY
TORTOISESHELL
TOYGER

Puzzle 33: Nationalities

```
G P N E A
A W H A S H S I K R U T
N R E S C E S E T L A M
A N N L I I N I J A I A
I G A U S T R A L I A N
T G R I T H T E P G C E
P M A E D S P O M A N Y
Y E F R E N C H C A J E
G         K I I S S R R
E
N
H
```

AMERICAN
AUSTRALIAN
EGYPTIAN
ENGLISH

FRENCH
GREEK
INDIAN
JAPANESE

MALTESE
SCOTTISH
TURKISH
WELSH

Puzzle 34: Putting on a Hat

```
L T T E R E B O
E L C L O D R B
T D A B Z E F R
A E T B R E A E
R K E B E R V C
I C M A O S I O
P O A D D T A W
S C E R R A T B
F F A I L L O O
E Z L P R K R Y
C O I B O W L E R R W R
R W Y T I T U R B A N T
```

AVIATOR
BASEBALL
BERET
BOWLER
CAP

COWBOY
DEERSTALKER
FEDORA
FEZ
PIRATE

SOMBRERO
TOP
TRILBY
TURBAN
WIZARD'S

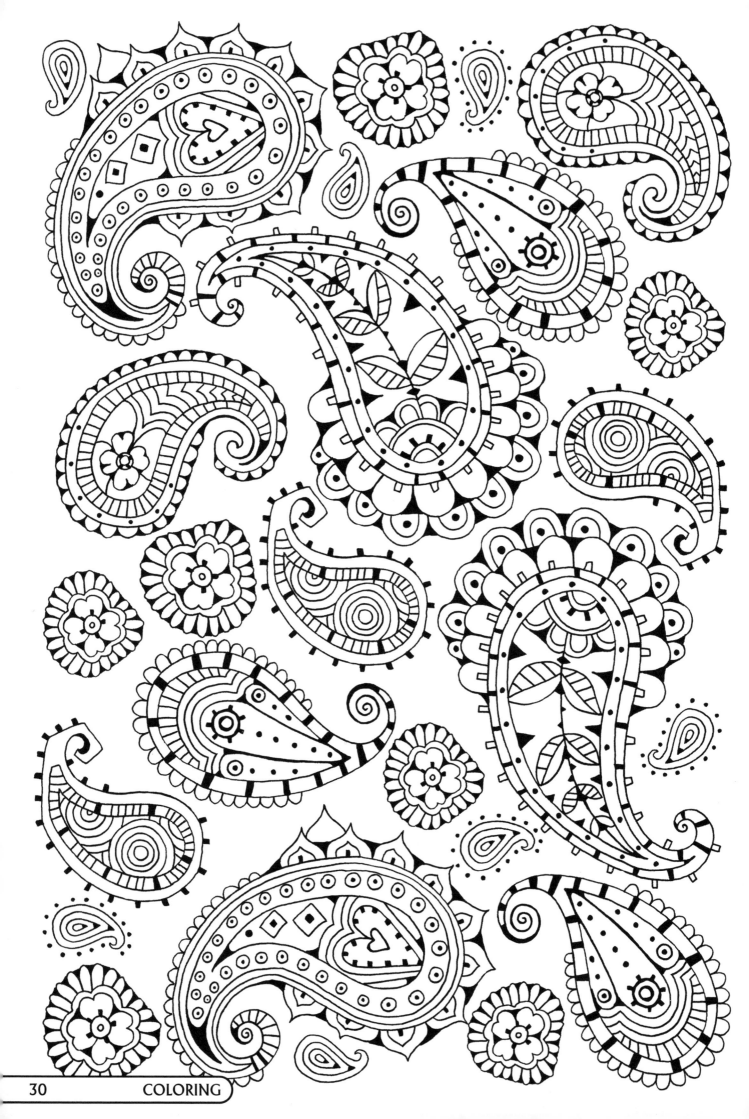

What will the divers discover?

Draw their horns.

Mine are curved.

Mine have knobs on the ends.

Mine are curly.

1 = yellow   2 = orange   3 = light blue   4 = pink   5 = light green

6 = dark blue   7 = red   8 = dark green   9 = brown

Draw the dragon's treasure.

DOODLING

Complete an incredible coral reef.

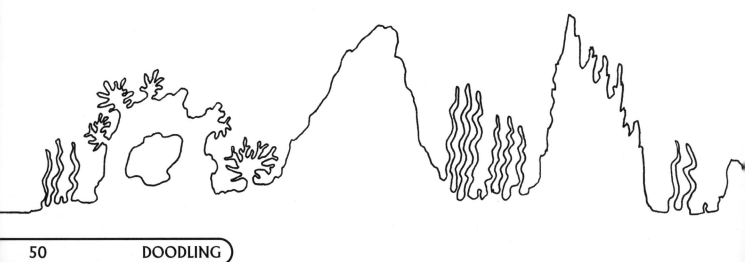

What is going on at the airport?

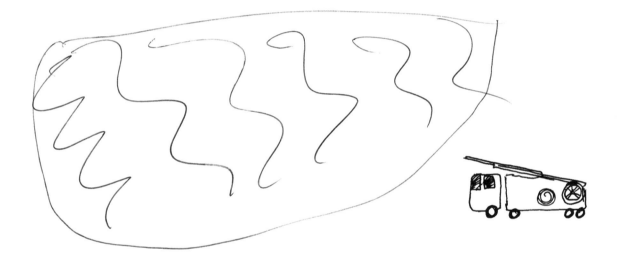

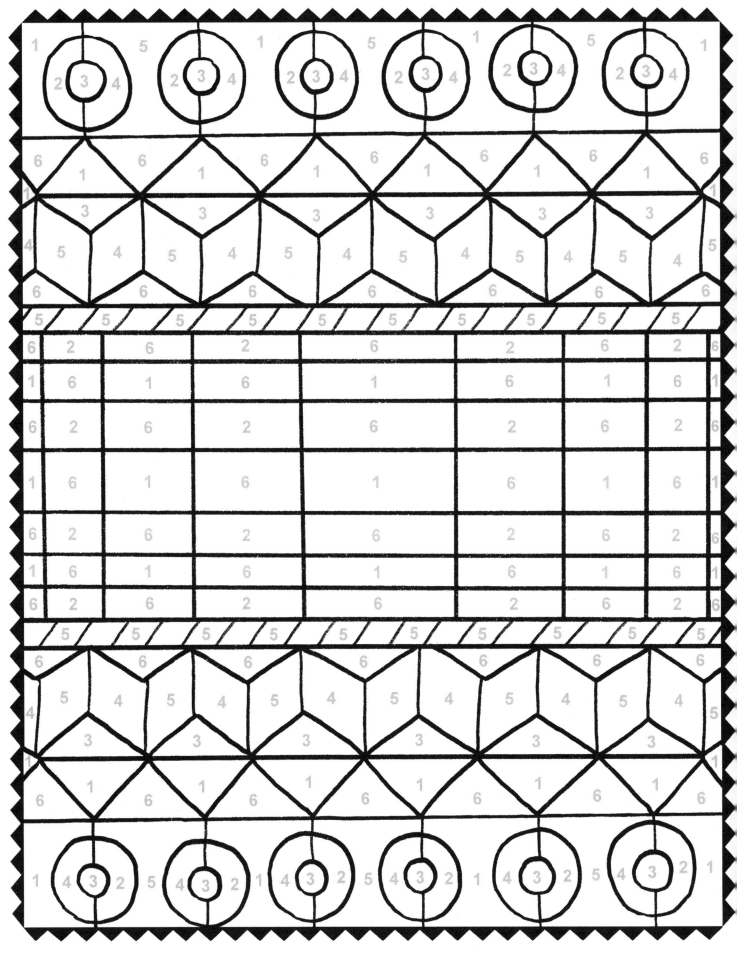

1 = blue   2 = orange   3 = red   4 = pink   5 = purple   6 = yellow

1 = yellow   2 = orange   3 = blue   4 = pink
5 = red   6 = purple   7 = light green   8 = dark green

Fill the field with bunnies.

DOODLING

Finish the fairy palace.

1 = yellow   2 = red   3 = blue   4 = purple   5 = pink   6 = orange

1 = dark green   2 = dark blue   3 = light green
4 = pink   5 = light blue   6 = purple   7 = yellow

Fill the field with wild flowers.

Create a sensational snowboarding jump.

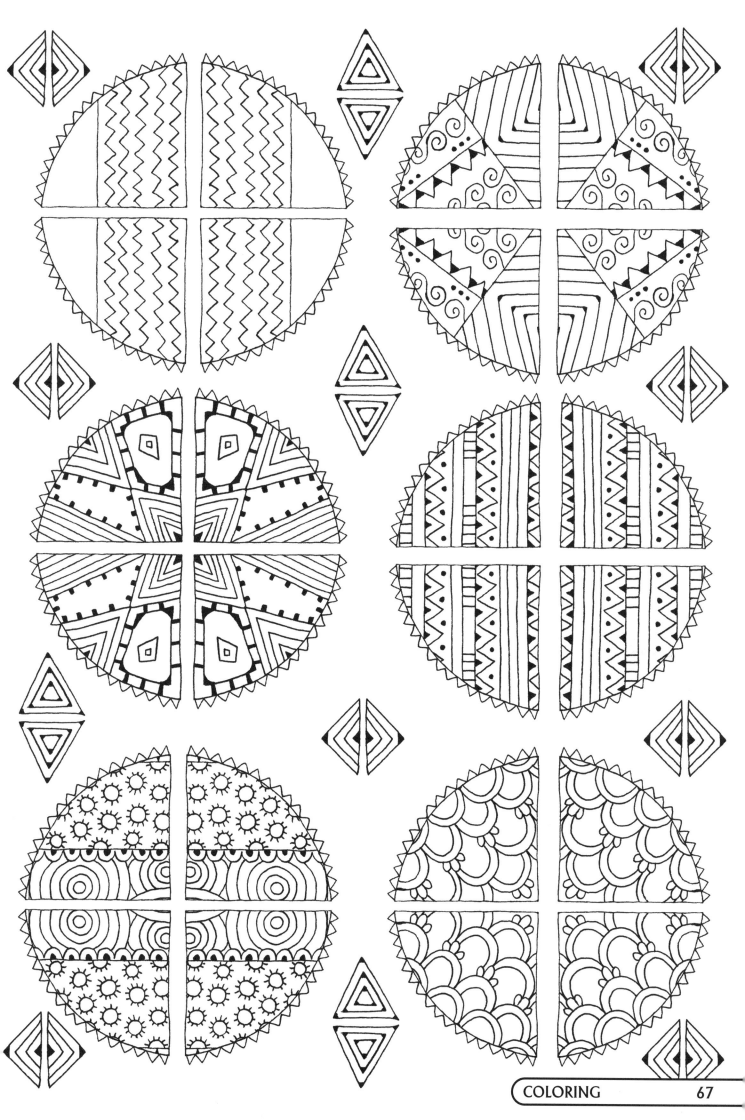

Giant digger!

DOODLING

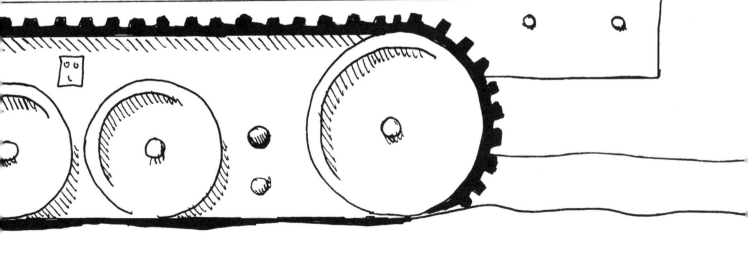

What is happening in the haunted house?

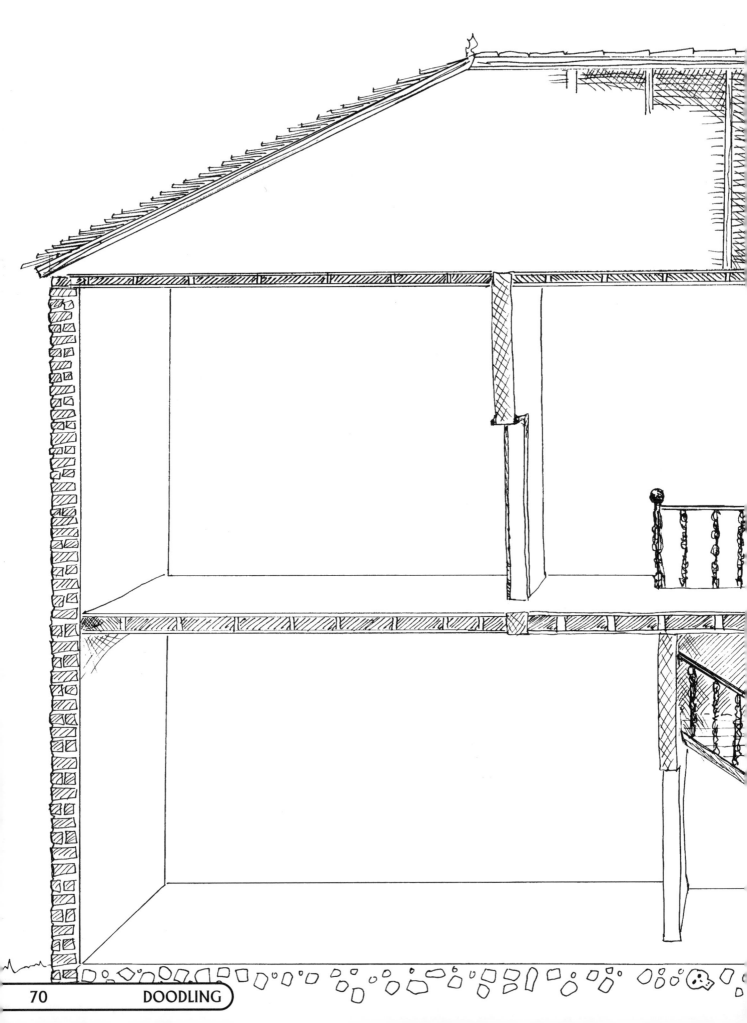

DOODLING

1 = orange
2 = yellow
3 = red
4 = grey
5 = purple
6 = blue
7 = green
8 = brown

Give these dogs the outfits they need.

I'm chilly. I need a warm coat and hat.

I need a fancy dress for a party.

I need a spooky Halloween costume.

I need a rain coat to stop me from getting wet.

DOT TO DOT

What has the pterodactyl caught?

potato

Ouch!

Decorate the skateboard.

1 = black
2 = pink

Your turn....

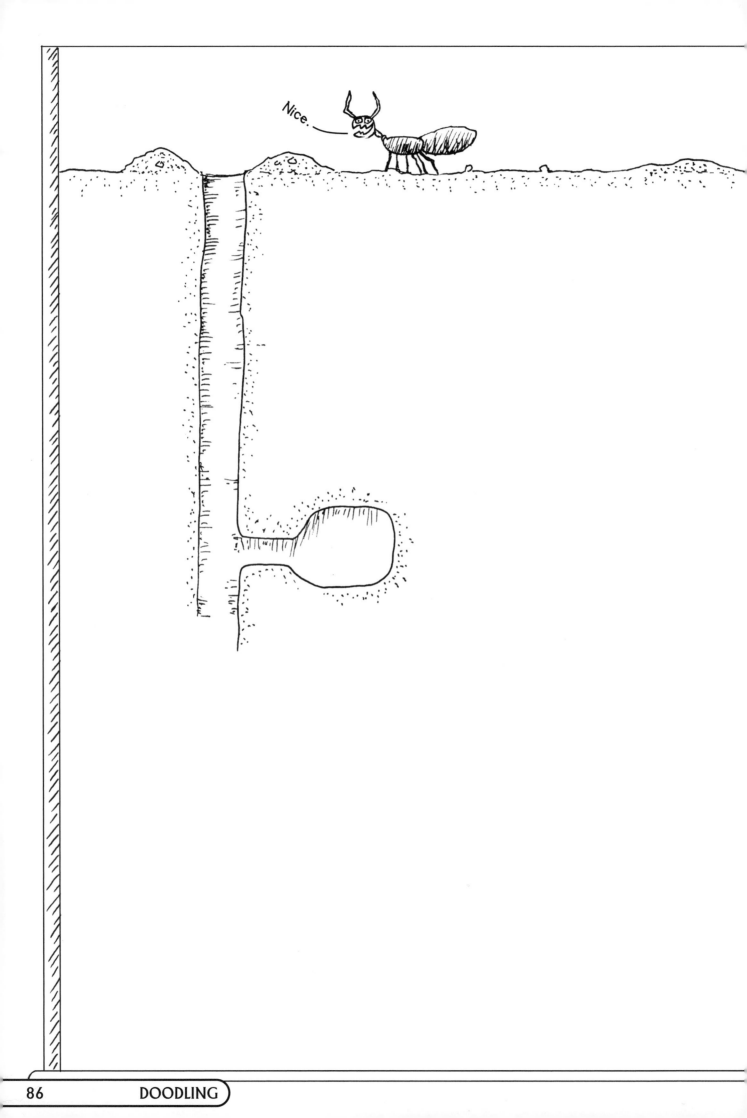

DOODLING

Finish the ant farm.

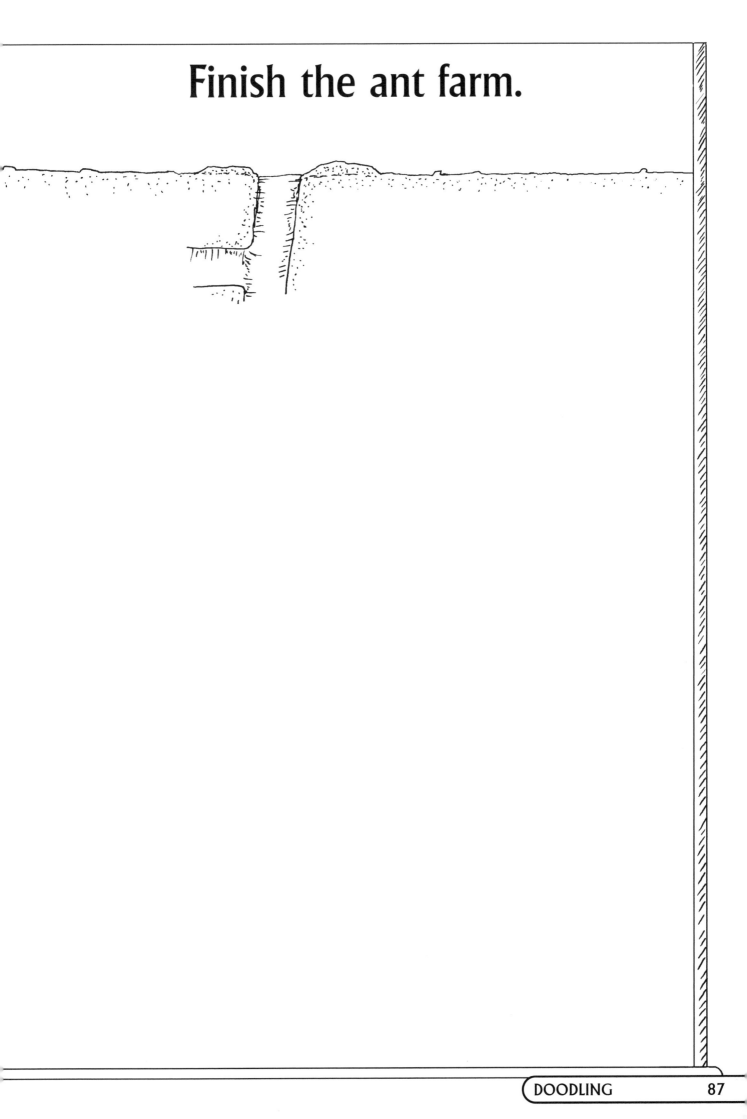

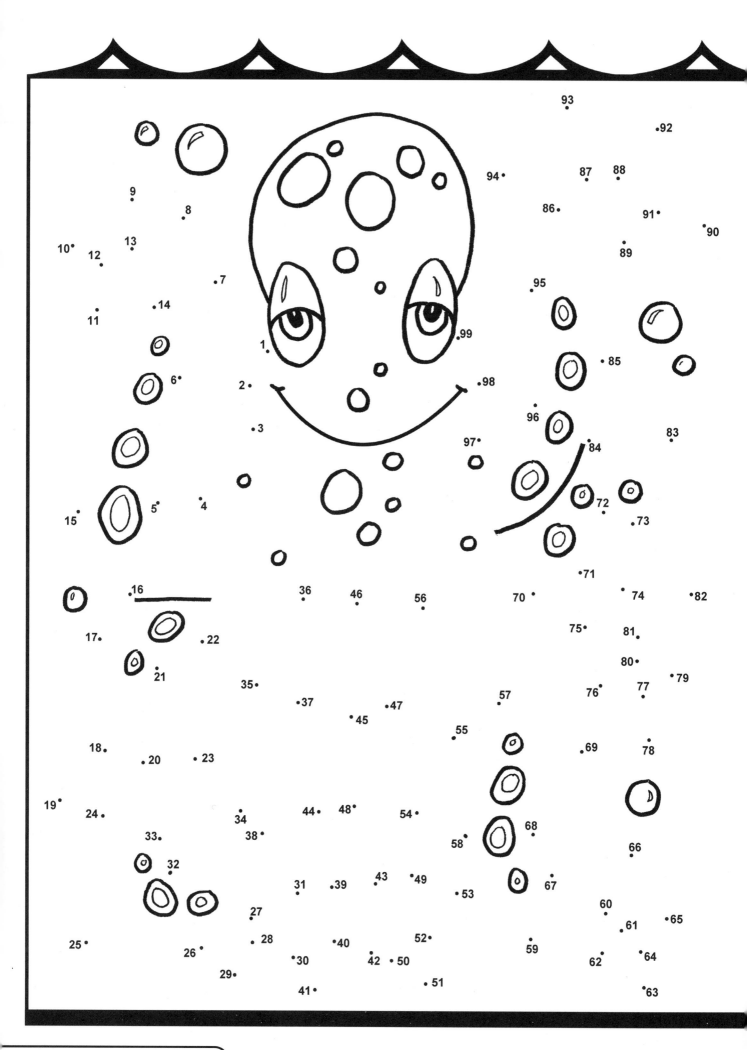

Fill in the savanna with animals.

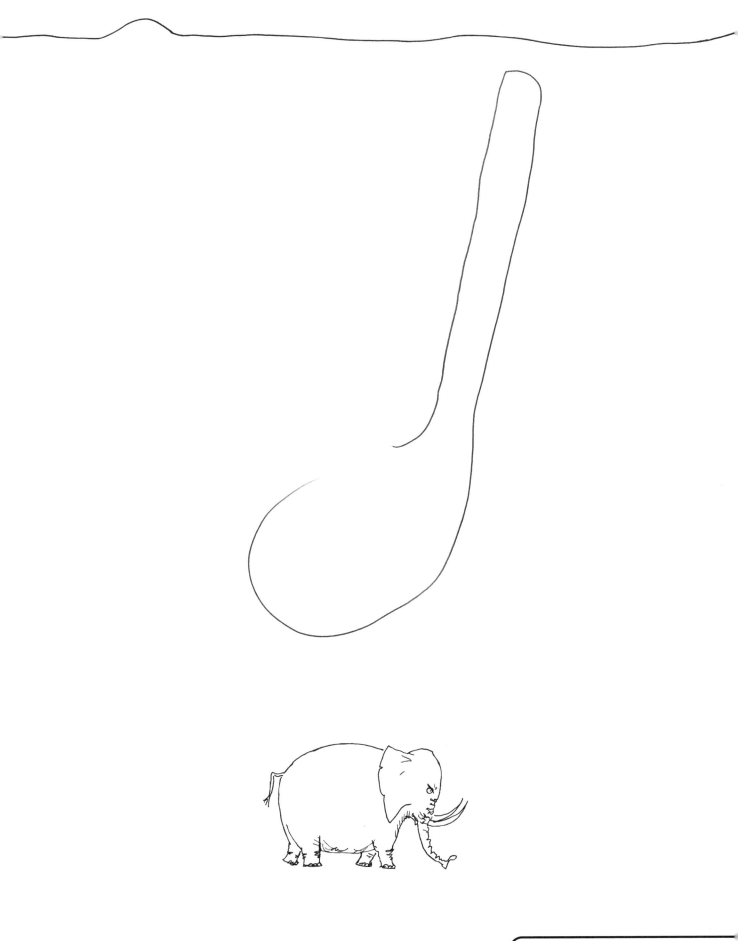

1 = red   2 = yellow   3 = orange

4 = green   5 = blue   6 = purple

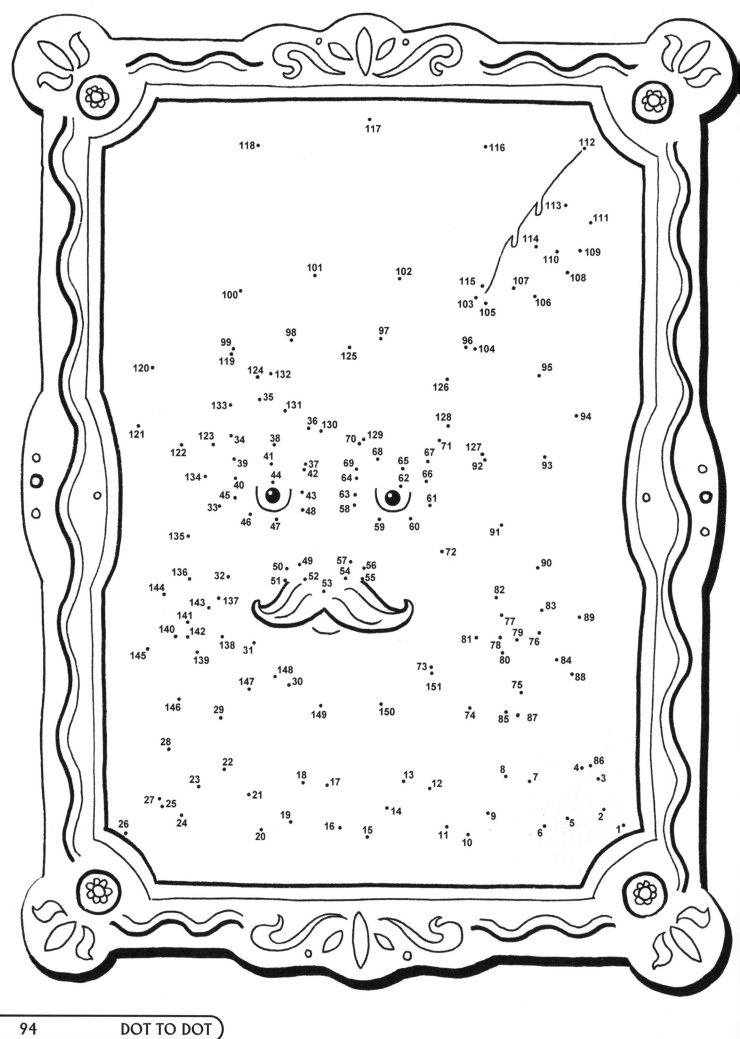

Finish the dinosaurs' footprints.

What's in the fish tank?

Doctor X-Ray says, "Draw their bones."

SUDOKU

The next section is full of Sudoku puzzles, a type of number puzzle that originated in Japan.

The overall aim is to fill in all the missing numbers in a grid. In a Sudoku grid, each row has nine squares, each column has nine squares, and each box has nine squares. When the puzzle is complete, every column, row and box must contain each of the numbers from 1 to 9, but only once.

In every Sudoku puzzle some of the numbers in the grid have been filled in already. You have to work out the numbers that go in each of the empty spaces.

The best way to start off solving a Sudoku puzzle is to look out for rows, columns, and boxes which have lots of numbers already filled in, as these are often the easiest to complete. Then you're well on your way to completing the whole puzzle!

If you get completely stuck and can't work out which number goes where, don't worry–all of the answers are in the back of the book.

Puzzle: 1

	5	1				8	4	
3	8	4		5		2	7	6
6	7	2				5	1	9
1	3	9	7		8	4	2	5
2			3	1	5			7
5	6	7	4		2	1	3	8
4	9	3				6	5	2
8	2	6		3		7	9	1
	1	5				3	8	

Puzzle: 2

4	8	2		9		5	3	1
3	7	1	8		5	6	2	9
9		6	1		2	4		7
2		7	3		9	1		8
			7					
5		3	4		8	7		2
6		5	9		1	8		3
7	3	9	5		4	2	1	6
1	2	8		6		9	5	4

Puzzle: 3

8		2				5		9
7	6	3	1	5		4	8	2
5	4	9		8	2	7	3	1
	3			1	4	6	5	
	9	4		2		3	1	
	5	8	7	3			9	
4	2	5	8	6		9	7	3
9	8	6		4	7	1	2	5
3		1				8		6

Puzzle: 4

	9	7				4	8	
2	8	5		9		1	3	7
1	3	4	7		2	9	6	5
	5	8	2	6	3	7	4	
			9	4	8			
	6	3	1	5	7	8	2	
8	2	9	3		6	5	1	4
5	4	1		2		3	7	6
	7	6				2	9	

Puzzle: 5

5	7	8				4	2	6
6	3	4	5		2	1	9	8
1		9				7		3
3	6	5		4		8	7	2
	8	2		5		9	3	
9	1	7		3		5	6	4
8		1				2		9
7	9	6	1		4	3	8	5
2	4	3				6	1	7

Puzzle: 6

8	9		4	3			2	6
	2	4	9	5	6	8	1	3
	3	5	2	8	1	4	9	7
	7	6		9			4	1
				1				
9	1			4		3	7	
1	6	2	5	7	8	9	3	
3	5	9	1	2	4	7	6	
4	8			6	9		5	2

Puzzle: 7

2	3	9		1	4	7	5	6
1	4	8	7	6		9	2	3
5	7			3		8	1	
4	9			8	3			2
	2			5			9	
6			4	2			8	7
	1	2		9			4	5
3	8	5			4	6	1	7
9	6	4	5	7		2	3	8

Puzzle: 8

1	2	3	4		6	7	5	8
9	4	5	1	7	8	2	6	3
	6	7	2	3	5	4	1	
	9						8	
		8		5		1		
	7						2	
	5	2	8	4	9	6	3	
3	8	6	7	2	1	9	4	5
4	1	9	5		3	8	7	2

Puzzle: 9

5	3	4				1	6	9
9	7	2	1		3	5	8	4
1		8				2		3
4	1	5	6		7	3	9	8
		7		1		4		
6	9	3	4		8	7	2	1
7		6				8		2
3	8	9	2		1	6	4	5
2	5	1				9	3	7

Puzzle: 10

4	2	9						3
	7	5		2			9	
3	6	1		5	9	8	7	2
1	8		7	6	2	9	4	5
6	5	7		4		3	2	8
9	4	2	3	8	5		1	6
7	1	4	2	3		5	8	9
	9			7		1	3	
5						2	6	7

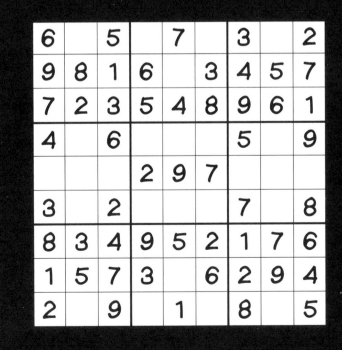

Puzzle: 11

8		5	3	2	7	1	4	6
		7	4					3
1		3		5		7	8	2
7	3	1	9	6		4	5	8
9		2		4		6		1
4	8	6		7	5	2	3	9
3	7	8		1		9		4
5					4	8		
2	1	4	7	9	8	3		5

Puzzle: 12

2	7	9	8	1	6	5		3
5	8	6		3	4	1	9	7
	4	1	7			6	2	8
6							1	5
8	3			7			6	2
1	2							9
7	1	8			3	2	5	
4	6	2	5	8		9	3	1
9		3	1	6	2	8	7	4

Puzzle: 13

2	7	9	1		5	3	8	6
	5	8				4	9	
3	4	6	9		2	7	5	1
	2		8	7	9		6	
7			6	2	4			8
	6		5	1	3		2	
9	8	2	7		1	6	4	3
	3	7				2	1	
4	1	5	2		6	8	7	9

Puzzle: 14

6		5		7		3		2
9	8	1	6		3	4	5	7
7	2	3	5	4	8	9	6	1
4		6				5		9
			2	9	7			
3		2				7		8
8	3	4	9	5	2	1	7	6
1	5	7	3		6	2	9	4
2		9		1		8		5

Puzzle: 15

9	5	3	6		8	4	7	2
6	8	2	4		7	5	3	1
	4	1	3	5	2	8	9	
	6			3			8	
			5	2	4			
	7			6			2	
	3	5	9	7	6	2	4	
8	2	6	1		3	9	5	7
4	9	7	2		5	6	1	3

Puzzle: 16

7		6	8	5	4	9		3
5	4	1	3	2		6	7	8
8	9	3	6	7	1	4		5
		8		4				1
		5		1		3		
6				8		5		
3		2	1	6	7	8	4	9
4	6	9		3	8	1	5	7
1		7	4	9	5	2		6

Puzzle: 17

	7	8	4	3	6	5	1	2
5	2	4	8	7		6	9	3
3	1	6						
	6	5		4		2	3	8
	9	7		2		1	4	
2	4	3		1		7	5	
						8	2	4
4	3	1		8	2	9	6	5
6	8	2	5	9	4	3	7	

Puzzle: 18

5	8						6	2
9	1	2	6		4	7	3	5
6	7	4	3	5	2	9	1	8
7	3			4			9	6
			7	9	5			
8	2			3			4	7
1	4	8	5	2	3	6	7	9
2	9	6	8		7	3	5	4
3	5						8	1

Puzzle: 19

9	5		7				2	8
7	8	3	1		2	9	4	5
6	2	4	8		9	3	1	7
		6	5		3	8		
2				4				1
		5	9		1	4		
1	9	2	3		6	5	7	4
3	6	7	4		5	2	8	9
5	4		2		7		6	3

Puzzle: 20

4	5	1	9		7	6	2	3
	9	3	4	1	6	5	7	
8	7	6	2	5	3	9	4	1
			3		5			
		4		2		3		
			1		8			
5	1	2	8	9	4	7	3	6
	4	7	5	3	2	8	1	
9	3	8	6		1	4	5	2

Puzzle: 21

7	5			9			8	6
2	6	9	1		8	3	4	5
8	1	3	6		5	9	2	7
	3		4		6		7	
4			3	1	2			9
	2		9		7		3	
5	4	8	7		1	2	9	3
3	7	6	8		9	5	1	4
1	9		3			6	8	

Puzzle: 22

8		2	7		9	1		4
3	5	7	6		1	8	2	9
1	9	4	8		5	3	6	7
			3		7			
2	3	1		6		4	7	5
			4		2			
7	4	3	2		6	5	9	1
6	1	9	5		4	2	8	3
5		8	1		3	7		6

Puzzle: 23

8	6	3	7		2	4	5	9
4	9	2	6		5	1	3	7
5	7						2	6
	5	8		3		2	6	
1			9	2	8			3
	2	7		5		9	4	
6	8						9	4
2	3	4	8		9	7	1	5
7	1	9	5		3	6	8	2

Puzzle: 24

1	4	9	7		6	3	8	2
6	5	2	4		3	1	7	9
	3	7		2		5	4	
		5	8		4	2		
2	1			9			3	8
		4	6		2	7		
	6	3		7		8	1	
4	2	8	3		1	9	5	7
5	7	1	9		8	6	2	3

Puzzle: 25

	9	7	1	6	3	8	5	
5	1	3	9		4	2	6	7
4	6	8	7	5	2	9	3	1
		2				1		
	4			3			8	
		6				3		
6	2	1	4	7	8	5	9	3
9	8	4	3		5	6	7	2
	3	5	6	2	9	4	1	

Puzzle: 26

2	3	6	9		1	7	5	8
	9	5		7		2	1	
7	1	8	5		3	4	6	9
		3	2	8	5	1		
			3	1	4			
		2	6	9	7	3		
5	2	9	7		8	6	4	1
	8	1		5		9	3	
3	7	4	1		9	8	2	5

Puzzle: 27

	8	1				7	3	
3	7	4	6		8	1	5	9
5	9	2				4	8	6
8	6	3	4		5	2	7	1
	1			6			4	
4	2	9	3		1	8	6	5
1	5	8				6	9	7
9	3	6	1		7	5	2	4
	4	7				3	1	

Puzzle: 28

3		1	5	2	6	4	9	8
	5	8		4	9		6	3
4		6	3	8	7	1	2	5
			7	5	1			
	1		8	6	3		7	
			2	9	4			
1	3	4	6	7	2	8		9
8	2		4	1		6	3	
7	6	5	9	3	8	2		1

Puzzle: 29

5	7	3	9	1	4	2	6	8
2	1	8	7		3	9	5	4
	4	9		5		7	3	
	8	4				5	1	
			4	8	1			
	2	6				8	4	
	3	2		4		1	8	
4	5	1	8		6	3	9	7
8	6	7	1	3	9	4	2	5

Puzzle: 30

4	6	8				3	2	9
3	2						1	7
1	7	5	2	3	9	6	4	8
9	8	2	5		1	7	3	6
				2				
5	3	4	8		7	2	9	1
8	5	6	3	9	4	1	7	2
7	9						6	4
2	4	1				9	5	3

Puzzle: 31

5	2	4	1	7	8	3	9	
9		3	2	6		5		
6	8	1	5	9	3		2	7
		5	3	4		6		8
		7		2		1		
1		8		5	7	2		
3	4		7	8	5	9	1	2
		9		3	2	7		5
	5	2	9	1	6	8	3	4

Puzzle: 32

6			5	1	3	4	7	8
1	5	4	8	6	7	3		2
3			9		2	6	5	1
2	4	1	7					
8			1	2	4			9
					8	1	2	4
5	1	3	6		9			7
4		8	2	3	5	9	1	6
9	2	6	4	7	1			3

Puzzle: 33

4	3	1				7	5	9
9		2		1		4		6
5	6	7	4		3	2	1	8
6	7	3				9	2	4
1	5			2			8	7
2	9	8				5	6	1
3	2	9	1		6	8	7	5
7		6		8		1		2
8	1	5				6	4	3

Puzzle: 34

2	9	3	7		1	6	5	8
5	4	8		3		1	7	9
6		1		9		2		4
7	8	2				5	4	1
			5	7	2			
9	3	5				7	6	2
4		9		2		3		5
3	5	7		8		4	2	6
8	2	6	3		4	9	1	7

Puzzle: 35

2	6	3	8	9		5	4	1
5	7	4	1	6			8	3
	1	8	4	3	5	2	7	6
			5			6		
8	9			1			2	5
	4			2				
6	8	1	2	4	3	7	5	
7	5			8	1	4	3	2
4	3	2		7	9	6	1	8

Puzzle: 36

6	3	2	9		1	5	7	4
7	5		2		4		3	9
9	8	4				2	1	6
1	6		5		7		9	2
			4	9	8			
5	4		6		2		8	3
3	2	7				9	6	8
8	9		3		6		4	7
4	1	6	8		9	3	2	5

Puzzle: 37

	4	3	7		2	9	8	
8	7	9	3		5	2	4	1
5	2	1	4		9	3	6	7
4			8	3	7			6
				2				
1			5	9	6			2
3	8	4	6		1	7	2	9
2	6	5	9		8	1	3	4
	1	7	2		3	6	5	

Puzzle: 38

5	3	6	7		1	8	9	2
8	1	7	3		2	6	4	5
	4	2		6		1	7	
		8	2	1	6	9		
			4	5	3			
		1	8	7	9	5		
	6	3		8		4	2	
2	9	5	6		4	7	8	1
1	8	4	9		7	3	5	6

Puzzle: 39

4	9		5	2	6		7	3
			9		8			
			3	4	7			
9		2				4		7
		7	4		3	2		
8		3				9		5
			1	7	9			
			2		5			
7	2		6	3	4		8	9

Puzzle: 40

		6				8		
8		7				4		5
3		4	5	8	1	7		6
	4	8				9	7	
			7		9			
	6	9				3	5	
6		3	2	9	5	1		7
1		5				6		2
		2				5		

Puzzle: 41

			9	5	6			
9			2		3			8
		3	4	7	8	1		
2	6						9	7
		7	8		2	5		
5	9						1	3
		2	1	6	4	9		
8			7		5			1
			3	8	9			

Puzzle: 42

3			8	2	9			5
	8		3	4	5		7	
	9		7		6		3	
		6				2		
9			6		2			7
		3				5		
	5		9		3		2	
	7		1	8	4		5	
6			2	5	7			4

Puzzle: 43

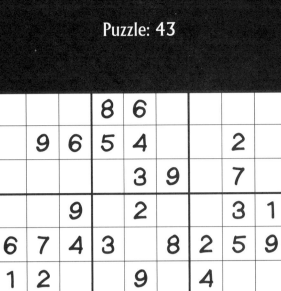

Puzzle: 44

	7	4				1	6	
8		6				2		5
	1	5		7		8	3	
		3	8		6	7		
	2						5	
		9	2		3	4		
	3	2		6		5	8	
9		8				6		1
	6	7				9	2	

Puzzle: 45

			3	8		5		
8	5		6	9		4		
			7	2				
3	2		9			1		
4	8	9	5		3	6	7	2
		6		8			3	5
			7	6				
	4		8	5			9	6
	6		9	4				

Puzzle: 46

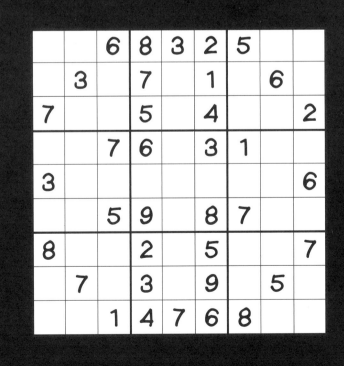

Puzzle: 47

			4	1				
	5		2	6		9	4	
	3			5	9			
		4		7			1	9
5	8	9	3		1	4	6	7
6	7			8		5		
			6	9			7	
	1	3		4	2		8	
				3	5			

Puzzle: 48

	2			7			1	
6		5		8		9		7
1				9				6
		8	9	2	7	6		
	9			8		5		4
		2	6	4	3	1		
9				5				1
2		1		3		5		9
	8			6			3	

Puzzle: 49

	2		8		5		7	
3			9		1			6
			4	7	6			
1		2	5		7	6		3
		8				2		
6		3	2		9	4		7
			1	5	8			
8			6		2			4
	6		7		3		1	

Puzzle: 50

		4		9			3	
	1	9		7	2	8		6
8				5	3	2		
			6	8	7			
	6		3		5		1	
			9	4	1			
		5	2	1				9
2		1	7	3		5	6	
	8			6		1		

Puzzle: 51

			5	9	1			
			2		6			
	5	9	7		4	2	6	
4		5	6		8	1		9
	2						4	
3		1	4		9	7		2
	4	3	9		7	6	5	
			8		2			
			3	4	5			

Puzzle: 52

	9	7		4		3		
				8				4
1		5		3		8		2
			4	2	8			
7	8	4	3		6	5	2	9
			9	5	7			
4		1		6		9		3
5				9				
		2		7		1	5	

Puzzle: 53

	2	9		3		5	6	
		8		6		7		
1			8	9	7			4
			5	4	2			
		5	7		3	9		
			9	8	6			
6			1	5	4			9
		4		2		6		
	9	1		7		2	4	

Puzzle: 54

8			3	1			2	
			4	5	8			
	5			9				7
	4		5	7	1	6	8	9
			8		9			
7	8	9	6	3	4		5	
1				5			6	
	5	1	6					
	6			8	7			1

All The
Answers

Crosswords pages 14-19

1
```
S A L M O N
W   A       I
H E L P F U L
    E       N
S P I N A C H
A   A   A   L
D A N G L E
```

2
```
    P R E S S
T O Y   C   I
I   R O L L S
N   A   I   T
S U M U P   E
E   I   S I R
L A D L E
```

3
```
      W
  C H A R T
  L   R   R
J O U R N A L
  C   I   C
  K N O C K
          R
```

4
```
E N J O Y   T
L         R O O F
F L O A T   R   A
  S   R   N   C
A S T R O N A U T
U   R   U   D
N   I   THORN
T I C K       E
    H   Q U I E T
```

5
```
  M   C A P E
H E R O   H
  R   N   A
  M A J O R
  A   U   A
  I   R O O M
I D L E   H
```

6
```
  C H E R R Y
  R   N     E
N O O D L E S
  W       A
U N D R E S S
S   A   E
E N A M E L
```

7
```
D U S K
I   P   S I R
S C O O P   E
C   O   R   M
U   KNIFE
S A Y   N   D
      U G L Y
```

8
```
  Q U A C K
  F   N   A
P A T I E N T
  L   F   C
S C O O T E R
  O   R   L
G N O M E
```

9
```
  M     C
  C A M E R A
F O R   A
  M E S S Y
  M   H O G
C O U P O N
  N   E
```

10
```
K   D I E T
L A C E   X
R   F   C
A P R I L
O   O   A
K   S O I L
Z E S T   M
```

11
```
  F O S S I L
  E   O   U
J E W E L   N
E   A   V   C
A   F R E S H
N   E   A
S O R R O W
```

12
```
H A R P
  B   R I P
  S   E   R
P O S T M A N
  R   E   Y
  B I N   E
      D A R E
```

13
```
  L   S   G
V E H I C L E
  T   L   A
S T R E T C H
  E   N   I
C R A C K E R
  S   E   R
```

14
```
  D   S
  P O L I C E
M U M   R
P E A C E
P   L A X
H E L I U M
  T   B
```

15
```
P   S I G N
P A T H   A
  N   U   R
  T O T A L
  H   T   A
  E   L U N G
T R E E   D
```

16
```
P R O M P T
  I   A   O
H E A V Y   A
A   W   O   S
P   F I R S T
P   U   O
Y E L L O W
```

17
```
  T   D
  C A R P E T
F O X   S
  P I X I E
  P   D R Y
S E C R E T
  R   A
```

18
```
R E C I P E
A   O   R
W E L C O M E
  L   M
S P E C I A L
  G   S   A
  C E L E R Y
```

19
```
C O P E
O   L   B Y E
L L A M A   A
U   N   R   R
M E L B O W
N U T   E   I
      D R A G
```

20
```
  U P S E T
  P   A   A
T O U R I S T
  L   A   T
G L A S S E S
  E   O   R
A N G L E
```

21
```
  W   I
M A R I N E
F A N   S
  S T A G E
  T   I C Y
D E P A R T
  R   L
```

22
```
    S
W H E E L
  I   R   A
A N T I Q U E
  D   O   G
Y O U T H
      S
```

Word Searches pages 21-29

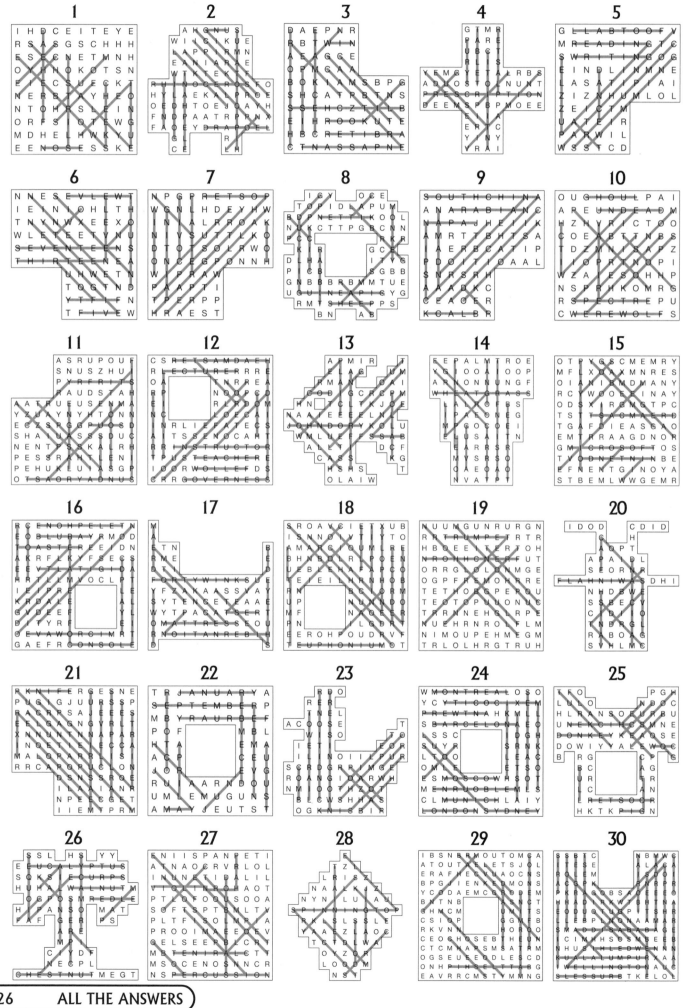